PERSONS IN THE PLAY

A Fool
A Blind Man
Cuchulain, King of Muirthemne
Conchubar
A Young Man, son of Cuchulain
Kings and Singing Women

A great hall at Dundealgan, not 'Cuchulain's great ancient house' but an assembly house nearer to the sea. A big door at the back, and through the door misty light as of sea-mist. There are many chairs and one long bench. One of these chairs, which is towards the front of the stage, is bigger than the others. Somewhere at the back there is a table with flagons of ale upon it and drinking-horns. There is a small door at one side of the hall. A Fool and Blind Man, both ragged, and their features made grotesque and extravagant by masks, come in through the door at the back. The Blind Man leans upon a staff.

FOOL. What a clever man you are though you are blind! There's nobody with two eyes in his head that is as clever as you are. Who but you could have thought that the henwife sleeps every day a little at noon? I would never be able to steal anything if you didn't tell me where to look for it. And what a good cook you are! You take the fowl out of my hands after I have stolen it and plucked it, and you put it into the big pot at the fire there, and I can go out and run races with the witches at the edge of the waves and get an appetite, and when I've got it, there's the hen waiting inside for me, done to the turn.

BLIND MAN [*who is feeling about with his stick*]. Done to the turn.

FOOL [*putting his arm round Blind Man's neck*]. Come now, I'll have a leg and you'll have a leg, and we'll draw lots for the wish-bone. I'll be praising you, I'll be praising you while we're eating it, for your good plans and for your good cooking. There's nobody in the world like you, Blind Man. Come, come. Wait a minute. I shouldn't have closed the door. There are some that look for me, and I wouldn't like them not to find me. Don't tell it to anybody, Blind Man. There are some that follow me. Boann herself out of the river and Fand out of the deep sea. Witches they are, and they come by in the wind, and they cry, 'Give a kiss, Fool, give a kiss', that's what they cry. That's wide enough. All the witches can come in now. I wouldn't have them beat at the door and say, 'Where is the Fool? Why has he put a lock on the door?' Maybe they'll hear the bubbling of the pot and come in and sit on the ground. But we won't give them any of the fowl. Let them go back to the sea, let them go back to the sea.

BLIND MAN [*feeling legs of big chair with his hands*]. Ah! [*Then, in a louder voice as he feels the back of it.*] Ah—ah—

FOOL. Why do you say 'Ah-ah'?

BLIND MAN. I know the big chair. It is to-day the High King Conchubar is coming. They have brought out his chair. He is going to be Cuchulain's master in earnest from this day out. It is that he's coming for.

FOOL. He must be a great man to be Cuchulain's master.

BLIND MAN. So he is. He is a great man. He is over all the rest of the kings of Ireland.

FOOL. Cuchulain's master! I thought Cuchulain could do anything he liked.

BLIND MAN. So he did, so he did. But he ran too wild, and Conchubar is coming to-day to put an oath upon him that will stop his rambling and make him as biddable as a house-dog and keep him always at his hand. He will sit in this chair and put the oath upon him.

FOOL. How will he do that?

BLIND MAN. You have no wits to understand such things. [*The Blind Man has got into the chair.*] He will sit up in this chair and he'll say: 'Take the oath, Cuchulain. I bid you take the oath. Do as I tell you. What are your wits compared with mine, and what are your riches compared with mine? And what sons have you to pay your debts and to put a stone over you when you die? Take the oath, I tell you. Take a strong oath.'

FOOL [*crumpling himself up and whining*]. I will not. I'll take no oath. I want my dinner.

BLIND MAN. Hush, hush! It is not done yet.

FOOL. You said it was done to a turn.

BLIND MAN. Did I, now? Well, it might be done, and not done. The wings might be white, but the legs might be red. The flesh might stick hard to the bones and not come away in the teeth. But, believe me, Fool, it will be well done before you put your teeth in it.

FOOL. My teeth are growing long with the hunger.

BLIND MAN. I'll tell you a story—the kings have story-tellers while they are waiting for their dinner—I will tell you a story with a fight in it, a story with a champion in it, and a ship and a queen's son that has his mind set on killing somebody that you and I know.

FOOL. Who is that? Who is he coming to kill?

BLIND MAN. Wait, now, till you hear. When you were stealing the fowl, I was lying in a hole in the sand, and I heard three men coming with a shuffling sort of noise. They were wounded and groaning.

ON BAILE'S STRAND

1904

By W. B. YEATS

To
William Fay
because of the beautiful fantasy of his
playing in the character of the Fool

A Digireads.com Book
Digireads.com Publishing

On Baile's Strand
By W. B. Yeats
ISBN 10: 1-4209-4160-7
ISBN 13: 978-1-4209-4160-9

This edition copyright © 2011

Please visit *www.digireads.com*

FOOL. Go on. Tell me about the fight.

BLIND MAN. There had been a fight, a great fight, a tremendous great fight. A young man had landed on the shore, the guardians of the shore had asked his name, and he had refused to tell it, and he had killed one, and others had run away.

FOOL. That's enough. Come on now to the fowl. I wish it was bigger, wish it was as big as a goose.

BLIND MAN. Hush! I haven't told you all. I know who that young man is. I heard the men who were running away say he had red hair, that he had come from Aoife's country, that he was coming to kill Cuchulain.

FOOL. Nobody can do that.

[*To a tune*]

>Cuchulain has killed kings,
>Kings and sons of kings,
>Dragons out of the water,
>And witches out of the air,
>Banachas and Bonachas and people of the woods.

BLIND MAN. Hush! hush!

FOOL [*still singing*].

>Witches that steal the milk,
>Fomor that steal the children,
>Hags that have heads like hares,
>Hares that have claws like witches,
>All riding a-cock-horse

[*Spoken*]

Out of the very bottom of the bitter black North.

BLIND MAN. Hush, I say!

FOOL. Does Cuchulain know that he is coming to kill him?

BLIND MAN. How would he know that with his head in the clouds? He doesn't care for common fighting. Why would he put himself out, and nobody in it but that young man? Now if it were a white fawn that might turn into a queen before morning—

FOOL. Come to the fowl. I wish it was as big as a pig; a fowl with goose grease and pig's crackling.

BLIND MAN. No hurry, no hurry. I know whose son it is. I wouldn't tell anybody else, but I will tell you,—a secret is better to you than your dinner. You like being told secrets.

FOOL. Tell me the secret.

BLIND MAN. That young man is Aoife's son. I am sure it is Aoife s son, it flows in upon me that it is Aoife's son. You have often heard me talking of Aoife, the great woman-fighter Cuchulain got the mastery over in the North?

FOOL. I know, I know. She is one of those cross queens that live in hungry Scotland.

BLIND MAN. I am sure it is her son. I was in Aoife's country for a long time.

FOOL. That was before you were blinded for putting a curse upon the wind.

BLIND MAN. There was a boy in her house that had her own red colour on him, and everybody said he was to be brought up to kill Cuchulain, that she hated Cuchulain. She used to put a helmet on a pillar-stone and call it Cuchulain and set him casting at it. There is a step outside—Cuchulain's step.

[*Cuchulain passes by in the mist outside the big door.*]

FOOL. Where is Cuchulain going?

BLIND MAN. He is going to meet Conchubar that has bidden him to take the oath.

FOOL. Ah, an oath, Blind Man. How can I remember so many things at once? Who is going to take an oath?

BLIND MAN. Cuchulain is going to take an oath to Conchubar who is High King.

FOOL. What a mix-up you make of everything, Blind Man! You were telling me one story, and now you are telling me another story. . . How can I get the hang of it at the end if you mix everything at the beginning? Wait till I settle it out. There now, there's Cuchulain [*he points to one foot*], and there is the young man [*he points to the other foot*] that is coming to kill him, and Cuchulain doesn't know. But where's Conchubar? [*Takes bag from side.*] That's Conchubar with all his riches—Cuchulain, young man, Conchubar.—And where's Aoife? [*Throws up cap.*] There is Aoife, high up on the mountains in high hungry Scotland. Maybe it is not true after all. Maybe it was your own making up. It's many a time you cheated me before with your lies. Come to the cooking-pot, my stomach is pinched and rusty. Would you have it to be creaking like a gate?

BLIND MAN. I tell you it's true. And more than that is true. If you listen to what I say, you'll forget your stomach.

FOOL. I won't.

BLIND MAN. Listen. I know who the young man's father is, but I won't say. I would be afraid to say. Ah, Fool, you would forget everything if you could know who the young man's father is.

FOOL. Who is it? Tell me now quick, or I'll shake you. Come, out with it, or I'll shake you.

[*A murmur of voices in the distance.*]

BLIND MAN. Wait, wait. There's somebody coming. . . . It is Cuchulain is coming. He's coming back with the High King. Go and ask Cuchulain. He'll tell you. It's little you'll care about the cooking pot when you have asked Cuchulain that . . .

[*Blind Man goes out by side door.*]

FOOL. I'll ask him. Cuchulain will know. He was in Aoife's country [*Goes up stage.*] I'll ask him. [*Turns and goes down stage.*] But, no, I won't ask him, I would be afraid. [*Going up again.*] Yes, I will ask him. What harm in asking? The Blind Man said I was to ask him. [*Going down.*] No, no. I'll not ask him. He might kill me. I have but killed hens and geese and pigs. He has killed kings. [*Goes up again almost to big door.*] Who says I'm afraid? I'm not afraid. I'm no coward. I'll ask him. No, no, Cuchulain, I'm not going to ask you.

        He has killed kings,
        Kings and the sons of kings,
        Dragons out of the water,
        And witches out of the air,
Banachas and Bonachas and people of the woods.

[*Fool goes out by side door, the last words being heard outside. Cuchulain and Conchubar enter through the big door at the back. While they are still outside, Cuchulain's voice is heard raised in anger. He is a dark man, something over forty years of age. Conchubar is much older and carries a long staff, elaborately carved or with an elaborate gold handle.*]

CUCHULAIN. Because I have killed men without your bidding
And have rewarded others at my own pleasure,
Because of half a score of trifling things,
You'd lay this oath upon me, and now—and now
You add another pebble to the heap,
And I must be your man, well-nigh your bondsman,
Because a youngster out of Aoife's country
Has found the shore ill-guarded.

CONCHUBAR. He came to land
    While you were somewhere out of sight and hearing,
    Hunting or dancing with your wild companions.

CUCHULAIN. He can be driven out. I'll not be bound.
    I'll dance or hunt, or quarrel or make love,
    Wherever and whenever I've a mind to.
    If time had not put water in your blood,
    You never would have thought it.

CONCHUBAR. I would leave
    A strong and settled country to my children.

CUCHULAIN. And I must be obedient in all things;
    Give up my will to yours; go where you please;
    Come when you call; sit at the council-board
    Among the unshapely bodies of old men;
    I whose mere name has kept this country safe,
    I that in early days have driven out
    Maeve of Cruachan and the northern pirates,
    The hundred kings of Sorcha, and the kings
    Out of the Garden in the East of the World.
    Must I, that held you on the throne when all
    Had pulled you from it, swear obedience
    As if I were some cattle-raising king?
    Are my shins speckled with the heat of the fire,
    Or have my hands no skill but to make figures
    Upon the ashes with a stick? Am I
    So slack and idle that I need a whip
    Before I serve you?

CONCHUBAR. No, no whip, Cuchulain,
    But every day my children come and say:
    'This man is growing harder to endure.
    How can we be at safety with this man
    That nobody can buy or bid or bind?
    We shall be at his mercy when you are gone;
    He burns the earth as if he were a fire,
    And time can never touch him.'

CUCHULAIN. And so the tale
    Grows finer yet; and I am to obey
    Whatever child you set upon the throne,
    As if it were yourself!

CONCHUBAR. Most certainly.
> I am High King, my son shall be High King;
> And you for all the wildness of your blood,
> And though your father came out of the sun,
> Are but a little king and weigh but light
> In anything that touches government,
> If put into the balance with my children.

CUCHULAIN. It's well that we should speak our minds out plainly,
> For when we die we shall be spoken of
> In many countries. We in our young days
> Have seen the heavens like a burning cloud
> Brooding upon the world, and being more
> Than men can be now that cloud's lifted up,
> We should be the more truthful. Conchubar,
> I do not like your children—they have no pith,
> No marrow in their bones, and will lie soft
> Where you and I lie hard.

CONCHUBAR. You rail at them
> Because you have no children of your own.

CUCHULAIN. I think myself most lucky that I leave
> No pallid ghost or mockery of a man
> To drift and mutter in the corridors
> Where I have laughed and sung.

CONCHUBAR. That is not true.
> For all your boasting of the truth between us;
> For there is no man having house and lands,
> That have been in the one family, called
> By that one family's name for centuries,
> But is made miserable if he know
> They are to pass into a stranger's keeping,
> As yours will pass.

CUCHULAIN. The most of men feel that,
> But you and I leave names upon the harp.

CONCHUBAR. You play with arguments as lawyers do
> And put no heart in them. I know your thoughts,
> For we have slept under the one cloak and drunk
> From the one wine-cup. I know you to the bone,
> I have heard you cry, aye, in your very sleep,
> 'I have no son', and with such bitterness
> That I have gone upon my knees and prayed
> That it might be amended.

CUCHULAIN. For you thought
    That I should be as biddable as others
    Had I their reason for it; but that's not true;
    For I would need a weightier argument
    Than one that marred me in the copying,
    As I have that clean hawk out of the air
    That, as men say, begot this body of mine
    Upon a mortal woman.

CONCHUBAR. Now as ever
    You mock at every reasonable hope,
    And would have nothing, or impossible things.
    What eye has ever looked upon the child
    Would satisfy a mind like that?

CUCHULAIN. I would leave
    My house and name to none that would not face
    Even myself in battle.

CONCHUBAR. Being swift of foot,
    And making light of every common chance,
    You should have overtaken on the hills
    Some daughter of the air, or on the shore
    A daughter of the Country-under-Wave.

CUCHULAIN. I am not blasphemous.

CONCHUBAR. Yet you despise
    Our queens, and would not call a child your own,
    If one of them had borne him.

CUCHULAIN. I have not said it.

CONCHUBAR. Ah! I remember I have heard you boast,
    When the ale was in your blood, that there was one
    In Scotland, where you had learnt the trade of war,
    That had a stone-pale cheek and red-brown hair;
    And that although you had loved other women,
    You'd sooner that fierce woman of the camp
    Bore you a son than any queen among them.

CUCHULAIN. You call her a 'fierce woman of the camp',
    For, having lived among the spinning-wheels,
    You'd have no woman near that would not say,
    'Ah! how wise!' 'What will you have for supper?'
    'What shall I wear that I may please you, sir?'
    And keep that humming through the day and night

　　　　For ever. A fierce woman of the camp!
　　　　But I am getting angry about nothing.
　　　　You have never seen her. Ah! Conchubar, had you seen her
　　　　With that high, laughing, turbulent head of hers
　　　　Thrown backward, and the bowstring at her ear,
　　　　Or sitting at the fire with those grave eyes
　　　　Full of good counsel as it were with wine,
　　　　Or when love ran through all the lineaments
　　　　Of her wild body—although she had no child,
　　　　None other had all beauty, queen or lover,
　　　　Or was so fitted to give birth to kings.

CONCHUBAR. There's nothing I can say but drifts you farther
　　　　From the one weighty matter. That very woman—
　　　　For I know well that you are praising Aoife—
　　　　Now hates you and will leave no subtlety
　　　　Unknotted that might run into a noose
　　　　About your throat, no army in idleness
　　　　That might bring ruin on this land you serve.

CUCHULAIN. No wonder in that, no wonder at all in that.
　　　　I never have known love but as a kiss
　　　　In the mid-battle, and a difficult truce
　　　　Of oil and water, candles and dark night,
　　　　Hillside and hollow, the hot-footed sun
　　　　And the cold, sliding, slippery-footed moon—
　　　　A brief forgiveness between opposites
　　　　That have been hatreds for three times the age
　　　　Of this long-'stablished ground.

CONCHUBAR. Listen to me.
　　　　Aoife makes war on us, and every day
　　　　Our enemies grow greater and beat the walls
　　　　More bitterly, and you within the walls
　　　　Are every day more turbulent; and yet,
　　　　When I would speak about these things, your fancy
　　　　Runs as it were a swallow on the wind.

　　　[*Outside the door in the blue light of the sea-mist are many old and young Kings;
　　　　amongst them are three Women, two of whom carry a bowl of fire. The third, in
　　　　what follows, puts from time to time fragrant herbs into the fire so that it flickers
　　　　up into brighter flame.*]

　　　　Look at the door and what men gather there—
　　　　Old counsellors that steer the land with me,
　　　　And younger kings, the dancers and harp-players
　　　　That follow in your tumults, and all these
　　　　Are held there by the one anxiety.

Will you be bound into obedience
And so make this land safe for them and theirs?
You are but half a king and I but half;
I need your might of hand and burning heart,
And you my wisdom.

CUCHULAIN [*going near to door*].
Nestlings of a high nest,
Hawks that have followed me into the air
And looked upon the sun, we'll out of this
And sail upon the wind once more. This king
Would have me take an oath to do his will,
And having listened to his tune from morning,
I will no more of it. Run to the stable
And set the horses to the chariot-pole,
And send a messenger to the harp-players.
We'll find a level place among the woods,
And dance awhile.

A YOUNG KING. Cuchulain, take the oath.
There is none here that would not have you take it.

CUCHULAIN. You'd have me take it? Are you of one mind?

THE KINGS. All, all, all, all!

A YOUNG KING. Do what the High King bids you.

CONCHUBAR. There is not one but dreads this turbulence
Now that they're settled men.

CUCHULAIN. Are you so changed,
Or have I grown more dangerous of late?
But that's not it. I understand it all.
It's you that have changed. You've wives and children now,
And for that reason cannot follow one
That lives like a bird's flight from tree to tree.—
It's time the years put water in my blood
And drowned the wildness of it, for all's changed,
But that unchanged.—I'll take what oath you will:
The moon, the sun, the water, light, or air,
I do not care how binding.

CONCHUBAR. On this fire
That has been lighted from your hearth and mine;
The older men shall be my witnesses,
The younger, yours. The holders of the fire
Shall purify the thresholds of the house

With waving fire, and shut the outer door,
According to the custom; and sing rhyme
That has come down from the old law-makers
To blow the witches out. Considering
That the wild will of man could be oath-bound,
But that a woman's could not, they bid us sing
Against the will of woman at its wildest
In the Shape-Changers that run upon the wind.

> [*Conchubar has gone on to his throne.*]

THE WOMEN. [*They sing in a very low voice after the first few words so that the others all but drown their words.*]

> May this fire have driven out
> The Shape-Changers that can put
> Ruin on a great king's house
> Until all be ruinous.
> Names whereby a man has known
> The threshold and the hearthstone,
> Gather on the wind and drive
> The women none can kiss and thrive,
> For they are but whirling wind,
> Out of memory and mind.
> They would make a prince decay
> With light images of clay
> Planted in the running wave;
> Or, for many shapes they have,
> They would change them into hounds
> Until he had died of his wounds,
> Though the change were but a whim;
> Or they'd hurl a spell at him,
> That he follow with desire
> Bodies that can never tire
> Or grow kind, for they anoint
> All their bodies, joint by joint,
> With a miracle-working juice
> That is made out of the grease
> Of the ungoverned unicorn.
> But the man is thrice forlorn,
> Emptied, ruined, wracked, and lost,
> That they follow, for at most
> They will give him kiss for kiss
> While they murmur, 'After this
> Hatred may be sweet to the taste'.
> Those wild hands that have embraced
> All his body can but shove
> At the burning wheel of love

Till the side of hate comes up.
Therefore in this ancient cup
May the sword-blades drink their fill
Of the home-brew there, until
They will have for masters none
But the threshold and hearthstone.

CUCHULAIN [*speaking, while they are singing*].
   I'll take and keep this oath, and from this day
   I shall be what you please, my chicks, my nestlings.
   Yet I had thought you were of those that praised
   Whatever life could make the pulse run quickly,
   Even though it were brief, and that you held
   That a free gift was better than a forced.—
   But that's all over.—I will keep it, too;
   I never gave a gift and took it again.
   If the wild horse should break the chariot-pole,
   It would be punished. Should that be in the oath?

[*Two of the Women, still singing, crouch in front of him holding the bowl over their heads. He spreads his hands over the flame.*]

   I swear to be obedient in all things
   To Conchubar, and to uphold his children.

CONCHUBAR. We are one being, as these flames are one:
   I give my wisdom, and I take your strength.
   Now thrust the swords into the flame, and pray
   That they may serve the threshold and the hearthstone
   With faithful service.

[*The Kings kneel in a semicircle before the two Women and Cuchulain, who thrusts his sword into the flame. They all put the points of their swords into the flame. The third Woman is at the back near the big door.*]

CUCHULAIN. O pure, glittering ones
   That should be more than wife or friend or mistress,
   Give us the enduring will, the unquenchable hope,
   The friendliness of the sword!—

[*The song grows louder, and the last words ring out clearly. There is a loud knocking at the door, and a cry of* 'Open! open!']

CONCHUBAR. Some king that has been loitering on the way.
   Open the door, for I would have all know
   That the oath's finished and Cuchulain bound,
   And that the swords are drinking up the flame.

[*The door is opened by the third Woman, and a Young Man with a drawn sword enters.*]

YOUNG MAN. I am of Aoife's country.

[*The Kings rush towards him. Cuchulain throws himself between.*]

CUCHULAIN. Put up your swords.
    He is but one. Aoife is far away.

YOUNG MAN. I have come alone into the midst of you
    To weigh this sword against Cuchulain's sword.

CONCHUBAR. And are you noble? for if of common seed,
    You cannot weigh your sword against his sword
    But in mixed battle.

YOUNG MAN. I am under bonds
    To tell my name to no man; but it's noble.

CONCHUBAR. But I would know your name and not your bonds.
    You cannot speak in the Assembly House,
    If you are not noble.

FIRST OLD KING. Answer the High King!

YOUNG MAN. I will give no other proof than the hawk gives
    That it's no sparrow!

[*He is silent for a moment, then speaks to all.*]

    Yet look upon me, kings.
    I, too, am of that ancient seed, and carry
    The signs about this body and in these bones.

CUCHULAIN. To have shown the hawk's grey feather is enough,
    And you speak highly, too. Give me that helmet.
    I'd thought they had grown weary sending champions.
    That sword and belt will do. This fighting's welcome.
    The High King there has promised me his wisdom;
    But the hawk's sleepy till its well-beloved
    Cries out amid the acorns, or it has seen
    Its enemy like a speck upon the sun.
    What's wisdom to the hawk, when that clear eye
    Is burning nearer up in the high air?

[*Looks hard at Young Man; then comes down steps and grasps Young Man by shoulder.*]

Hither into the light.

[To Conchubar.]

The very tint
Of her that I was speaking of but now.
Not a pin's difference.

[To Young Man.]

You are from the North,
Where there are many that have that tint of hair—
Red-brown, the light red-brown. Come nearer, boy,
For I would have another look at you.
There's more likeness—a pale, a stone-pale cheek.
What brought you, boy? Have you no fear of death?

YOUNG MAN. Whether I live or die is in the gods' hands.

CUCHULAIN. That is all words, all words; a young man's talk.
　I am their plough, their harrow, their very strength;
　For he that's in the sun begot this body
　Upon a mortal woman, and I have heard tell
　It seemed as if he had outrun the moon
　That he must follow always through waste heaven,
　He loved so happily. He'll be but slow
　To break a tree that was so sweetly planted.
　Let's see that arm. I'll see it if I choose.
　That arm had a good father and a good mother,
　But it is not like this.

YOUNG MAN. You are mocking me;
　You think I am not worthy to be fought.
　But I'll not wrangle but with this talkative knife.

CUCHULAIN. Put up your sword; I am not mocking you.
　I'd have you for my friend, but if it's not
　Because you have a hot heart and a cold eye,
　I cannot tell the reason. *[To Conchubar.]*
　He has got her fierceness,
　And nobody is as fierce as those pale women.
　But I will keep him with me, Conchubar,
　That he may set my memory upon her
　When the day's fading.—You will stop with us,
　And we will hunt the deer and the wild bulls;
　And, when we have grown weary, light our fires
　Between the wood and water, or on some mountain

    Where the Shape-Changers of the morning come.
    The High King there would make a mock of me
    Because I did not take a wife among them.
    Why do you hang your head? It's a good life:
    The head grows prouder in the light of the dawn,
    And friendship thickens in the murmuring dark
    Where the spare hazels meet the wool-white foam.
    But I can see there's no more need for words
    And that you'll be my friend from this day out.

CONCHUBAR. He has come hither not in his own name
    But in Queen Aoife's, and has challenged us
    In challenging the foremost man of us all.

CUCHULAIN. Well, well, what matter?

CONCHUBAR. You think it does not matter,
    And that a fancy lighter than the air,
    A whim of the moment, has more matter in it.
    For, having none that shall reign after you,
    You cannot think as I do, who would leave
    A throne too high for insult.

CUCHULAIN. Let your children
    Re-mortar their inheritance, as we have,
    And put more muscle on.—I'll give you gifts,
    But I'd have something too—that arm-ring, boy.
    We'll have this quarrel out when you are older.

YOUNG MAN. There is no man I'd sooner have my friend
    Than you, whose name has gone about the world
    As if it had been the wind; but Aoife'd say
    I had turned coward.

CUCHULAIN. I will give you gifts
    That Aoife'll know, and all her people know,
    To have come from me. [*Showing cloak.*]
    My father gave me this.
    He came to try me, rising up at dawn
    Out of the cold dark of the rich sea.
    He challenged me to battle, but before
    My sword had touched his sword, told me his name,
    Gave me this cloak, and vanished.
    Say that I heard
    A raven croak on the north side of the house
    And was afraid.

CONCHUBAR. Witchcraft has troubled his mind.

CUCHULAIN. No witchcraft. His head is like a woman's head
　　I had a fancy for.

CONCHUBAR. A witch of the air
　　Can make a leaf confound us with memories.
　　They run upon the wind and hurl the spells
　　That make us nothing, out of the invisible wind.
　　They have gone to school to learn the trick of it.

CUCHULAIN. No, no—there's nothing out of common here;
　　The winds are innocent.—That arm-ring, boy.

A KING. If I've your leave I'll take this challenge up.

ANOTHER KING. NO, give it me, High King, for this wild Aoife
　　Has carried off my slaves.

ANOTHER KING. No, give it me,
　　For she has harried me in house and herd.

ANOTHER KING. I claim this fight.

OTHER KINGS [*together*].
　　And I! And I! And I!

CUCHULAIN. Back! back! Put up your swords! Put up your swords!
　　There's none alive that shall accept a challenge
　　I have refused. Laegaire, put up your sword!

YOUNG MAN. NO, let them come. If they've a mind for it,
　　I'll try it out with any two together.

CUCHULAIN. That's spoken as I'd have spoken it at your age.
　　But you are in my house. Whatever man
　　Would fight with you shall fight it out with me.
　　They're dumb, they're dumb. How many of you would meet [*Draws sword.*]
　　This mutterer, this old whistler, this sand-piper,
　　This edge that's greyer than the tide, this mouse
　　That's gnawing at the timbers of the world,
　　This, this—Boy, I would meet them all in arms
　　If I'd a son like you. He would avenge me
　　When I have withstood for the last time the men
　　Whose fathers, brothers, sons, and friends I have killed
　　Upholding Conchubar, when the four provinces
　　Have gathered with the ravens over them.
　　But I'd need no avenger. You and I
　　Would scatter them like water from a dish.

YOUNG MAN. We'll stand by one another from this out.
　Here is the ring.

CUCHULAIN. NO, turn and turn about.
　But my turn's first because I am the older.
　[*Spreading out cloak.*] Nine queens out of the Country-under-Wave
　Have woven it with the fleeces of the sea
　And they were long embroidering at it.—Boy,
　If I had fought my father, he'd have killed me,
　As certainly as if I had a son
　And fought with him, I should be deadly to him;
　For the old fiery fountains are far off
　And every day there is less heat o' the blood.

CONCHUBAR [*in a loud voice*].
　No more of this. I will not have this friendship.
　Cuchulain is my man, and I forbid it.
　He shall not go unfought, for I myself—

CUCHULAIN. I will not have it.

CONCHUBAR. You lay commands on me?

CUCHULAIN [*seizing Conchubar*].
　You shall not stir, High King. I'll hold you there.

CONCHUBAR. Witchcraft has maddened you.

THE KINGS [*shouting*]. Yes, witchcraft! witchcraft!

FIRST OLD KING. Some witch has worked upon your mind, Cuchulain.
　The head of that young man seemed like a woman's
　You'd had a fancy for. Then of a sudden
　You laid your hands on the High King himself!

CUCHULAIN. And laid my hands on the High King himself?

CONCHUBAR. Some witch is floating in the air above us.

CUCHULAIN. Yes, witchcraft! witchcraft! Witches of the air!
　[*To Young Man.*] Why did you? Who was it set you to this work?
　Out, out! I say, for now it's sword on sword!

YOUNG MAN. But. . . but I did not.

CUCHULAIN. Out, I say, out, out!

[*Young Man goes out followed by Cuchulain. The Kings follow them out with confused cries, and words one can hardly hear because of the noise. Some cry, 'Quicker, quicker!' 'Why are you so long at the door?' 'We'll be too late!' 'Have they begun to fight?' 'Can you see if they are fighting?' and so on. Their voices drown each other. The three Women are left alone.*]

FIRST WOMAN. I have seen, I have seen!

SECOND WOMAN. What do you cry aloud?

FIRST WOMAN. The Ever-living have shown me what's to come.
THIRD WOMAN. How? Where?

FIRST WOMAN. In the ashes of the bowl.

SECOND WOMAN. While you were holding it between your hands?

THIRD WOMAN. Speak quickly!

FIRST WOMAN. I have seen Cuchulain's roof-tree
    Leap into fire, and the walls split and blacken.

SECOND WOMAN. Cuchulain has gone out to die.

THIRD WOMAN. O! O!

SECOND WOMAN. Who could have thought that one so great as he
    Should meet his end at this unnoted sword!

FIRST WOMAN. Life drifts between a fool and a blind man
    To the end, and nobody can know his end.

SECOND WOMAN. Come, look upon the quenching of this greatness.

[*The other two go to the door, but they stop for a moment upon the threshold and wail.*]

FIRST WOMAN. No crying out, for there'll be need of cries
    And rending of the hair when it's all finished.

[*The Women go out. There is the sound of clashing swords from time to time during what follows. Enter the Fool, dragging the Blind Man.*]

FOOL. You have eaten it, you have eaten it! You have left me nothing but the bones.

[*He throws Blind Man down by big chair.*]

BLIND MAN. O, that I should have to endure such a plague! O, I ache all over! O, I am pulled to pieces! This is the way you pay me all the good I have done you.

FOOL. You have eaten it! You have told me lies. I might have known you had eaten it when I saw your slow, sleepy walk. Lie there till the kings come. O, I will tell Conchubar and Cuchulain and all the kings about you!

BLIND MAN. What would have happened to you but for me, and you without your wits? If I did not take care of you, what would you do for food and warmth?

FOOL. You take care of me? You stay safe, and send me into every kind of danger. You sent me down the cliff for gulls' eggs while you warmed your blind eyes in the sun; and then you ate all that were good for food. You left me the eggs that were neither egg nor bird. [*Blind Man tries to rise; Fool makes him lie down again.*] Keep quiet now, till I shut the door. There is some noise outside— a high vexing noise, so that I can't be listening to myself. [*Shuts the big door.*] Why can't they be quiet? Why can't they be quiet? [*Blind Man tries to get away.*] Ah! you would get away, would you? [*Follows Blind Man and brings him back.*] Lie there! lie there! No, you won't get away! Lie there till the kings come. I'll tell them all about you. I will tell it all. How you sit warming yourself, when you have made me light a fire of sticks, while I sit blowing it with my mouth. Do you not always make me take the windy side of the bush when it blows, and the rainy side when it rains?

BLIND MAN. O, good Fool! listen to me. Think of the care I have taken of you. I have brought you to many a warm hearth, where there was a good welcome for you, but you would not stay there; you were always wandering about.

FOOL. The last time you brought me in, it was not I who wandered away, but you that got put out because you took the crubeen out of the pot when nobody was looking. Keep quiet, now!

CUCHULAIN [*rushing in*]. Witchcraft! There is no witchcraft on the earth, or among the witches of the air, that these hands cannot break.

FOOL. Listen to me, Cuchulain. I left him turning the fowl at the fire. He ate it all, though I had stolen it. He left me nothing but the feathers.

CUCHULAIN. Fill me a horn of ale!

BLIND MAN. I gave him what he likes best. You do not know how vain this Fool is. He likes nothing so well as a feather.

FOOL. He left me nothing but the bones and feathers. Nothing but the feathers, though I had stolen it.

CUCHULAIN. Give me that horn. Quarrels here, too! [*Drinks.*] What is there between you two that is worth a quarrel? Out with it!

BLIND MAN. Where would he be but for me? I must be always thinking—thinking to get food for the two of us, and when we've got it, if the moon is at the full or the tide on the turn, he'll leave the rabbit in the snare till it is full of maggots, or let the trout slip back through his hands into the stream.

[*The Fool has begun singing while the Blind Man is speaking.*]

FOOL [*singing*].

> When you were an acorn on the tree-top,
> Then was I an eagle-cock;
> Now that you are a withered old block,
> Still am I an eagle-cock.

BLIND MAN. Listen to him, now. That's the sort of talk I have to put up with day out, day in.

[*The Fool is putting the feathers into his hair. Cuchulain takes a handful of feathers out of a heap the Fool has on the bench beside him, and out of the Fool's hair, and begins to wipe the blood from his sword with them.*]

FOOL. He has taken my feathers to wipe his sword. It is blood that he is wiping from his sword.

CUCHULAIN [*goes up to door at back and throws away feathers*]. They are standing about his body. They will not awaken him, for all his witchcraft.

BLIND MAN. It is that young champion that he has killed. He that came out of Aoife's country.

CUCHULAIN. He thought to have saved himself with witchcraft.

FOOL. That Blind Man there said he would kill you. He came from Aoife's country to kill you. That Blind Man said they had taught him every kind of weapon that he might do it. But I always knew that you would kill him.

CUCHULAIN [*to the Blind Man*]. You knew him, then?

BLIND MAN. I saw him, when I had my eyes, in Aoife's country.

CHULAIN. YOU were in Aoife's country?

BLIND MAN. I knew him and his mother there.

CUCHULAIN. He was about to speak of her when he died.

BLIND MAN. He was a queen's son.

CUCHULAIN. What queen? what queen? [*Seizes Blind Man, who is now sitting upon the bench.*] Was it Scathach? There were many queens. All the rulers there were queens.

BLIND MAN. No, not Scathach.

CUCHULAIN. It was Uathach, then? Speak! speak!

BLIND MAN. I cannot speak; you are clutching me too tightly. [*Cuchulain lets him go.*] I cannot remember who it was. I am not certain. It was some queen.

FOOL. He said a while ago that the young man was Aoife's son.

CUCHULAIN. She? No, no! She had no son when I was there.

FOOL. That Blind Man there said that she owned him for her son.

CUCHULAIN. I had rather he had been some other woman's son. What father had he? A soldier out of Alba? She was an amorous woman—a proud, pale, amorous woman.

BLIND MAN. None knew whose son he was.

CUCHULAIN. None knew! Did you know, old listener at doors?

BLIND MAN. No, no; I knew nothing.

FOOL. He said a while ago that he heard Aoife boast that she'd never but the one lover, and he the only man that had overcome her in battle. [*Pause.*]

BLIND MAN. Somebody is trembling, Fool! The bench is shaking. Why are you trembling? Is Cuchulain going to hurt us? It was not I who told you, Cuchulain.

FOOL. It is Cuchulain who is trembling. It is Cuchulain who is shaking the bench.

BLIND MAN. It is his own son he has slain.

CUCHULAIN. 'Twas they that did it, the pale windy people.
  Where? where? where? My sword against the thunder!
  But no, for they have always been my friends;
  And though they love to blow a smoking coal
  Till it's all flame, the wars they blow aflame
  Are full of glory, and heart-uplifting pride,
  And not like this. The wars they love awaken
  Old fingers and the sleepy strings of harps.
  Who did it then? Are you afraid? Speak out!
  For I have put you under my protection,
  And will reward you well. Dubthach the Chafer?
  He'd an old grudge. No, for he is with Maeve.

Laegaire did it! Why do you not speak?
What is this house?
[*Pause.*] Now I remember all.

[*Comes before Conchubar's chair, and strikes out with his sword, as if Conchubar was sitting upon it.*]

'Twas you who did it—you who sat up there
With your old rod of kingship, like a magpie
Nursing a stolen spoon. No, not a magpie,
A maggot that is eating up the earth!
Yes, but a magpie, for he's flown away.
Where did he fly to?

BLIND MAN. He is outside the door.

CUCHULAIN. Outside the door?

BLIND MAN. Between the door and the sea.

CUCHULAIN. Conchubar, Conchubar! the sword into your heart!

[*He rushes out. Pause. Fool creeps up to the big door and looks after him.*]

FOOL. He is going up to King Conchubar. They are all about the young man. No, no, he is standing still. There is a great wave going to break, and he is looking at it. Ah! now he is running down to the sea, but he is holding up his sword as if he were going into a fight. [*Pause.*] Well struck! well struck!

BLIND MAN. What is he doing now?

FOOL. O! he is fighting the waves!

BLIND MAN. He sees King Conchubar's crown on every one of them.

FOOL. There, he has struck at a big one! He has struck the crown off it; he has made the foam fly. There again, another big one!

BLIND MAN. Where are the kings? What are the kings doing?

FOOL. They are shouting and running down to the shore, and the people are running out of the houses. They are all running.

BLIND MAN. You say they are running out of the houses? There will be nobody left in the houses. Listen, Fool!

FOOL. There, he is down! He is up again. He is going out in the deep water. There is a big wave. It has gone over him. I cannot see him now. He has killed kings and giants, but the waves have mastered him, the waves have mastered him!

BLIND MAN. Come here, Fool!

FOOL. The waves have mastered him.

BLIND MAN. Come here!

FOOL. The waves have mastered him.

BLIND MAN. Come here, I say.

FOOL [*coming towards him, but looking backwards towards the door*]. What is it?

BLIND MAN. There will be nobody in the houses. Come this way; come quickly! The ovens will be full. We will put our hands into the ovens.

[*They go out.*]

THE END

Lightning Source UK Ltd.
Milton Keynes UK
UKOW02f1916200115

244809UK00001B/85/P